The Stone of Language

the Stone *of* Language

Anya Achtenberg

West End Press

Acknowledgments

"Torturer's Resignation" won First Prize in *Another Chicago Magazine's* Poetry 2000 contest, and appeared in the Fall 2000 issue.

"River Lament for Those Who Knew Derek" was finalist in the 1998 Allen Ginsberg Poetry Awards sponsored by the Poetry Center at Passaic County Community College, and it appeared in the *Paterson Literary Review* in 1999.

"Mother is carried off" appeared in *Blue Mesa Review* in 1998.

"Questions of War" appeared in *Rooster Crows at Light from the Bombing: Echoes from the Gulf War*, an anthology of poems and essays published by Inroads Press, 1992.

"Genesis" appeared in *Life on the Line: Selections on Words and Healing*, an anthology of poetry and prose published by Negative Capability Press, 1992.

"Elegy" appeared in *VISIONS-International* in 1991. It also appeared in Spanish translation as "Elegia" in the 1991 issue of *Punto 7*.

"February" appeared in *Pivot* in 1996.

"The Beginning of Night" appeared in the Spring 1990 issue of *Caprice*.

"Tirza in the Land of Numbers," "The Street of the Lost Child," and "Shoes" appeared in the July-August 1990 issue of *American Poetry Review*.

"These Snapshots I Have Lost," a finalist for the 1990 Pollak Prize, was published in the Spring 1990 issue of *The Madison Review*.

"Breath" won the Guy Owen Poetry Prize and appeared in the Fall 1989 issue of *Southern Poetry Review*.

"Occupations" won Honorable Mention in the 1989 Chester H. Jones National Poetry Competition and appeared in the anthology of winning poems.

"Man Behind a Store Window" appeared in *Ailanthus*, Winter 1986.

© 2004 by Anya Achtenberg
Printed in the United States of America

First edition July 2004
ISBN: 0-9753486-1-2

Book and cover design by Nancy Woodard

West End Press • P.O. Box 27334 • Albuquerque NM 87125

Contents

City Poem for Hanuman, the Monkey Scribe   1

Entrance
    Breath   3

The Beginning of Night
    The Beginning of Night   5
    4A, Brooklyn   6
    February   8
    Genesis   9
    News at the End of the Sky   11

Occupations
    Occupations   13
    Man Behind a Store Window in Spring   14
    Shoes   16
    Work Abroad: Riddles   17
    Commerce: Boys   20
    Torturer's Resignation   21
    Performers at Cirque du Soleil   22
        i.   Contortionists   22
        ii.   The Strong Man   23
        iii.   Clown Trotting in His Horse Costume   24
        iv.   Lady in White   25
    "They are there, their song is there"   26

Immigrants
    Brixton Photo   29
    Burning   31
    Immigrants   32
        i.   Looking for the Angel   32
        ii.   Story   32
        iii.   Change   33
        iv.   Immigrants   33
        v.   Return   34
        vi.   Counting   36
        vii.   Flight   37
        viii. History   38

The Street of the Lost Child

    The Street of the Lost Child   41

    Elegy   42

    Paraplegia   43

    River Lament for Those Who Knew Derek   45

    Notes on a Phone Call   46

    When We Can't Speak   47

    Mother Is Carried Off   50

These Snapshots I Have Lost

    "The woman seated made a sign of death"   53

    These Snapshots I Have Lost   55

    Questions of War   61

    From September 11   65

        i.   The Fall   65

        ii.   The Climb   66

        iii.   The Burial   67

    Easter Heart   69

The Stone of Language

    Disappointment Island   71

    Tirza in the Land of Numbers   72

    crush   75

    The Stone of Language   77

Notes   83

For those who "no longer remember . . .
That they used to be children
And once fed on light."*

For those who do.

And for the wanderers, the exiled,
who make a home in language.

*from "Brejo da Cruz" by Chico Buarque of Brazil

City Poem for Hanuman, the Monkey Scribe

You write in darkness under
eclipsed sun, black moon, collapsed stars.
You write by glow of catastrophe
with ink of river,
pen melting in flames
driving cries to paper.
You scramble over rubble
to the one breath still rising,
pull him to the top
and hiss life into his skull,
then dip your tail into
the bubble of his blood
and disappear
to write of it.

The cameras have missed you
but mark his crimson work pants,
his satin flesh, the falling knees
of helmeted helpers
as broken beams crash across
a hundred twenty-fifth street
to accuse another
vacant building trembling with shadows,
with confused lingering spirits,
while half a city crouches in the dust
below its windows, makes fires
in the mesh of garbage, cooks
what the other half has left,
and beats on the pavement
a history of journey.

The city is falling.
You who know shadow, blood and spirit
hang at its edge in silence,
tail fur bloody, shrill chatter buried,
grim pouch on a tattered tree by the river.
Still, you will write.
Ink is abundant
and will not stop flowing.

ENTRANCE

Breath

This is an ode to my breath
that circles the body and its stutter,
its ache and bend,
its opening and its bloodfall, its upheaval
and the long string of pleasure that falls from it
and is woven into the eye and hand of memory.
This is an ode to the darkness behind my eyes,
to the green pit that has darkened
and left its shell in the cellar of night.
This is the time when the flowers come forth
to suck at my lips, and the honey
that passes between us
is a soft whisper bathing the ear
in moisture and heat.
This is the night
when the spine becomes the straight road
of the body, up to the head
and down to the place of hushed entrance.
These are the fingertips that split open
and were healed, that stroke the life
into things, and mend,
stitch by stitch, that which has been
torn apart. This is a blessing
of feet, their bones and veins,
the splendid edifice of toes
huddled against each other.
This is an ode to the breath,
excited, tender, steady, musical,
warm and hushed, raising its open mouth
to all that may fall from the sky—
a blessing be upon its soft and shining name.

THE BEGINNING OF NIGHT

The Beginning of Night

When the cold came into her crib
she shook in its arms. The white
moon slipped in too, illuminating
her face till all saw, all the chorus
of stars roaring and shining
above her darkness,
and birds on the wing
flew past, brushing
her throat, and insects
marched over her belly and across
her eyelids.

She could not move
or cry out in the cold rain.
The late weak dawn trembled on the ceiling.
The neighbors crouched listening.
It was all cold and her
ice feet wept
under the thin cover
in their bare silence.

4A, Brooklyn

Why is she here, this street, this number,
between seagulls and the roar of trash?
How far can she pedal, can she run,
before her breath, extinguished, rises
to her throat and will not go down
to the cave where it flowers?
What marked the spot, built her into
the brick, another piece that fit,
arm caught in a slot,
leg caught behind her, always
stepping back, the perfect dance
away from the ledge?
She folds herself into the small cot
under the faceless shade
and its eclipse of the wild geometry
of night, whose dark heart
beats in her eye and ear,
in the chorus of refusal built into the floorplan
of each project apartment, refusal
in the kitchen, in the bedroom,
refusal on either side
of the triple-locked door
with its joker of peephole,
stranger on the outside, locked-up heart within.
The blind joker's eye sees
who comes to the door with circulars,
who stumbles, or drags, with a bottle, a bag,
who sheathes a blade when he notices,
rolls the white bag in his pocket,
returns with a shadow from the staircase
where he lay his heart and its beats
inside the tight fit of a frightened girl.

Why is she here, east of New York
and the blind-blaze sun,
skirting gangs of boys
in the ragweed lots?
How many will stand in front of her,
not letting her pass,
shoulder to shoulder in their common work
of helping her silence grow?

This is how she grows, here,
who she is burning out in her,
while her mother, holding up a small
mirror to see the back of her hairdo,
does not notice the misplaced pin,
but only her eye, without makeup, gazing back,
her daughter, frightened, beyond her,
holding her heart's blood closed,
and the semen, the knife and the sweet powders
that pull the shade down tighter.

Before the woman puts down the mirror,
she hears the pipes knock with life,
lets the shower's steam blur
the bathroom mirror
and the pocket mirror, the size of a face, she is holding,
and the last thing she sees is her own eye
before the eyelid of steam shuts

and she kneels on the cold tile
and holds a towel over her face
for a long time.

February

I see them, vicious, the children
on the ice, pulling
each other down, aiming
at the soft center of the other,
at the heart, at the stomach,
at the sex, and bursting
with all the strength of their new muscles
against the thin paper of skin,
new and ready to be written on
with the scars and harsh shadows
of their lives on earth among the others.
I see them from my window, all
sliding down the knife blade of the ice,
etching in that country of glass
their fury at the other just ahead,
that one with blue hat or red scarf.
They see the wild color of bird,
they fling themselves, they scream,
and the harsh light of their screams
batters my window as I remember
the child that I was, always
hit in the dark center,
in my dream,
in my light blue hat flying
up to the clouds.

Genesis

She sat on the stoop and looked out at all that had been made.
The heavens glimmered through black smoke
the vegetation withered as it struggled through concrete
and fat pink earthworms wriggled blind,
cut in two by boys with army knives.

Her father worked all night at the factory
and slept in the day when she was awake
so she had to be very quiet
and wait for the school bus outside on the stoop.
She tried not to be in the house alone when her father woke up
because sometimes he thought she was her mother.

She knew what he wanted
and didn't want to make him mad
but each time it happened
she could see a sad crazy bird fly past the window
and hurl itself into the river.

That day she stared down from the stoop
at an earthworm severed from itself,
one part inching toward the stubbly grass
and the other careening down the sidewalk
without its second half,
its cut end exposed for the first time to the world.
Then she remembered
she had left her science book on the table
near where the coats hung in a row.

When she entered, all light fled.
When he grabbed her, she fled further into the darkness,
and his voice was not soft and the fruit was not sweet
and she had not been able to name it for a long time.

She came back into the light
with her book and her bruised mouth
and rushed into the big yellow bus before it pulled away.
Then the sky opened up,
the storm's strength lodged the bleeding halves of earthworms
between the blades of stubbly grass,

and she decided to tell.
She saw each face
of each child in the bus like someone she used to be,
and the darkness broke in the sky
as the yellow bus pulled up to the school.

Then she clearly heard,
as she stood on her thin legs in front of the teacher,
her own voice work its way into the air.

News at the End of the Sky

Hold on, magic one,
your wild hair swamp sinking
into the bright feathers of dancing birds,
dancing on the living tendril.
Hold on when the deep etched bark
becomes you.
You are not all night
shadows that knife their way
into the faces of trees.
Hold on, magic one,
there, shining, at the end
of the dull and muddied sky
are the stars you must feed on,
and with this diet of shining
you will become someone's child,
held, spoken for,
named.
Hold on to this air that is the same
inside all of us and can tell
all our stories, hold on
to the immense silence that turns away from you
as you beg on your knees
beneath her velvet breast.

When you feel yourself
sucked into the fine point of the cone
of someone else's nightmare,
hold on
in the cawing that shreds wind,
in the stabbing of siren,
in the pounding of hammer
that shatters bone, eye, thought,
loveliness of child, twelve or thirteen,
carried in from the hallway
with her hand up, perhaps forever,
over her eyes.

Hold on, little magic one.
You are a bird.
Fly away.

Hold on
little one

hold on

OCCUPATIONS

Occupations

In the light rain, a man
sits on a crate stained
by the juice of the fruits he sorts,
good from bad, perfect
from too ripe, gone bad, won't do.
He is there every night, but tonight
he looks at me, his hands continue the work
he does not need his eyes for, and I say
Good night, though it isn't, and feel his eyes
try to decide what kind I am.
I give him my swayed sorry back
and my bare nervous hands
that count, weigh, and wrap
wedding rings all night in sleep
as they do all day in the factory.
Perhaps my hands would welcome the sweet pulp,
the yielding skin of the fruit his fingers know,
perhaps he desires the cold shining
hoops that roll out to the grand or shabby or
quick weddings in every part of the city. Perhaps
our hands would work best in each other's grasp
or palms up to the light rain, or palms down
on our chests, rising and falling
with the wind that moves gently through
the good lung and the bad,
as we dream of stillness, of our hands at peace,
as we dream of sleep, unbroken
sleep and the fruit
whose yielding skin breaks open
only for those who were there
at the beginning of its sweetness.

Man Behind a Store Window in Spring

Handbags strung under an awning
like so many plump birds on a branch,
melodic, grasping, clasps tight,
swaying above the barter for them,
and sullen mangos, quick notes
of lemons rolling,
jícama, yuca, plátano, pupusa,
merengue pumping, shaking the flayed
flanks of fish, the hips
of young mothers, baby
carriages wild with tantrums,
reefer and the sweet burning
of young hands to touch
what they have seen.

A young man listens, half, to instructions.
His open palms receive
tiny blossoms of pants, abbreviated shirts,
socks and underwear rolled, prenatal, in plastic.
He stares over his hands through the glass,
sees the girls in the streets and beyond,
dressed, naked, glass, cloth,
in his open hands, under leaden skies.
The mannequins, half-dressed,
stare at his thigh.
They call him to come back,
leave the girls who toss black hair
as they round the corner
into that animal breath that waits for them.
Come back and bend to the children, cover them,
button their little white shirts as they watch,
unblinking,
so his hands smooth the fabric
over their unyielding circles of waist,
but his eyes hunt beyond the glass.

At six, he leaves the store
and cannot remember what day it is.
When he hits the corner the sky opens,
whale belly up over the Palisades.
He sees the bridge, arc of light,
span the silence of water, the dim hopes of fish.
There's regular traffic over her,
heartbeat, breath,
the feet of a man who never stops running,
and a wave of air smacks against him,
pulls the hair back from his forehead,
as some giant sleeping
animal expels its breath
before it turns over
into the earth.

Shoes

These shoes are from Mexico. They are black, filled with the darkness of my step, like anyone's shoes. They are of a fine leather, soft and pliable. Their nights in hiding, their nights of emptiness, are much longer than the few hours in which they are filled, warm and purposeful, in motion, dancing perhaps, arriving somewhere. For those many hours, they are unseen, lying in the sad bottom of the closet or in the dusty corner of a back room, the toes pointed each in towards the other, in shyness or in fear. I cannot say that I have brought them with me wherever I have traveled, or when I have rested alongside another animal of this world. I cannot say they will be with me when I push through the groaning door, only that I have filled and emptied them like any master. For this I am ashamed, that I have left them forgotten when something else touched me and held me, and that they haven't much life without me. I am sorry for all this, but they are not blameless. In their emptiness, their empty mouths seem to say nothing else but to call out for me, and for this I am not guilty, or at least I am not the only guilty one here. And I know that for all their subservience, all their need, they will not accompany me as my feet of flesh vanish to bone, jointed filigree and deep shadow, rather, they will swim away through the darkness, fall right off the wire of my step. For this I curse them, leave them at night, thrust my feet into them violently when I can, when they will be surprised and feel pain in the delicate places where they are sewn together. I knew their unfaithfulness from the first moment I stepped out with them. But I've shown them who's boss, at least on this earth, and when we walk it is I who bear down on them, crush them a bit into the earth, into hard asphalt when we are in the city on business, and they can only respond by holding me tighter around the wide band of my toes, and by lying down beneath me each time I demand it. This power is only of this earth, but it will carry me, it will carry me.

Work Abroad: Riddles

The Thai woman sits behind
a display window
between folded limbs
of other women, a yellow pin
with a price over her breast.
Buddha looks on from his shrine
next to the snacks.
Half hour with a blue pin woman
is more expensive, but not much.
What invasion gathers here
to wrench these limbs apart,
leave them quivering
on the lumpy bed of assault?

This is the marketplace, free trade.
There are laws, theft is punished.
There are memories combed into
the hair of each woman.
There is a blues
in the chorus of eyes
against the red wall,
hair blows beneath the tiny
fan, there is heat.

There is family among them, they are
orphans sold by a mother or father
for refrigerator, TV, next meal,
to half a million men laying heavily
on top, day and night, endless moons,
endless blood,
endless punishment for the falling of
blood—a loss to business,
and for sins of disobedience
and laziness, for closed legs
and seamed sore mouth, for cradling
the head of the next woman
in her arms while a student waits,
getting drunk in the Angel Cafe,

deciding on the red or blue or yellow
or clear tag, until she grabs
the small silk purse
and steps out to peer
through the showcase window.

How much invasion remains, left behind
by soldiers who liked the smallness
of the women, who thought them lovely
and called them gooks, who needed
their smallness to feel their own
cruel dimensions, who did much killing?

How ancient
is the woman
in the doorway,
how many
sisters
does she have,
what masters
must she tend,
bound
to what gods?

Was she created for use,
slapped open, bought open,
left open and eyeless
to the constant landscape above her
—the fears of her invaders?
The marketplace flutters its awnings above,
blotting out sky
blotting out ocean shrunk to its salt
and to spines of dying fish.

The Thai woman behind the glass
knows love
is forbidden.
No outside man. No inside man. No
caress outside the exchange
for hard currency. No
soaring of hearts

in the thrill of bodies, no
pleasure that cannot
be bought with another.
No sunrise,
streetlights always shining
through store windows,
tags fluttering like heartbeats,
price of mother, daughter, sister,
painted for the drunk and the sober,
the scarred and the pampered,
who browse and measure, bargain
and agree, slide worn bills
between someone's breasts.
The tags that flutter do not
make a sound.

Who will buy a woman, or parts of a woman,
the sacred parts: soft fire of the temple,
breasts of life, the whisper behind her eyes,
her dreaming hands, the ancient animal that shadows her,
tongue of her cries, light she reaches for?
Who will buy her mother a refrigerator,
save her sister
from the same business,
who will buy her
after a good meal, know her
and know nothing, take her
and have nothing?
What will he buy,
what will he hold in his arms?
What dead trophy, what anger,
what product of a great machine,
what loss?

All is loss here: to buy loss, to come loss,
to come in her loss, to suck
loss, to dream loss, all is loss and everything
behind a window that waits, frozen by need,
will never be owned, even though it is bought,
and will never be lost,
though it has already been sold.

Commerce: Boys

In the forest, on the hilltop,
at the crossroads, heaps of stone
watch over us, protect
when stranger passes stranger
or stops to exchange a few words
or trade water for bread.
Blade sheathed, rock of death
thrown down, snarl and fist relaxed,
robbery, rape and murder
wait silently
beneath robes of night,
god of the crossroads holding open
the magical space for each
to pass through
another's life protected.

In the Milwaukee summer of '91
protection fails for those still boys,
Black, Asian, poor.
One, Laotian, lured
into the foul-smelling house,
runs outside into clothed daylight
and falls, naked and bereft of the hills
of his homeland, beneath the feet
of upright men,
bleeding from his buttocks
in a flesh heap on the concrete
to mark the crossing of police
and murderer, and the police look down
at his angles of bone, and his murderer
looks down at his angles of bone,
and something is agreed upon,
some value, some price, another secret
still bleeding,
and they walk away, clubs and guns quiet,
handcuffs swinging from leather belts,
as Jeffrey, blood in his fair hair,
drags the boy and his fourteen years
back up porchsteps into slaughterhouse,
his bones to meet the bones of
other strangers.

Torturer's Resignation

From all of this I am the only one who leaves.
The shadow of blood does not leave, nor the hands,
nor the child turned into a rope, nor the rope into fire,
nor the flame become plague of scattering and landlessness.

What is on the floor remains the stench of concrete,
what is wooden tilts forever into earth's loneliness,
what flies off is hair, what sings is only
feet burning like drums, what lights the way
is ordinary lampshade.

I am leaving the arc of rage.
I am leaving the covenant of bitter women.
I am leaving my birth into sin and the scalding purifications,
the scream of ceremony, that eats of the fruit
between our legs.

Armies of blind cloth, I'm going. Unmap me. I am leaving
the tunnel of agony that opens to be fed.
I am leaving the arm raised in the field of arms
over the thud of child, of grace, of song.

I leave all of this for a naked dance, for innocence
in my cousin's tent, for lunch with strangers and the fruit
of grenades blossoming only in the target of dreams.
I walk away like a man or like a woman.
My soldiers are the armies of fruit
in the market crates, spilling, rolling,
lime and mango singing.

Electric night, I leave you.
Animal incision and insect crawl,
green slip of bile and exhausted organs
waiting in the breathless river for one kiss or one note,
one dead mother, one gasping father,
for the probing of the sister of teeth and locked closets,
of blankets of shadow and postcards of blame,
I leave you, hood of nightmare, for breath, for air,
for an entire body.

The first line is borrowed from César Vallejo's poem "Paris, October 1936."

Performers at Cirque du Soleil

i.   Contortionists

Tiny sisters, one slightly older, moon
at her shoulder, glow of god in the crook
of the tent. In the blink of an eye, their spines
doubled over. One's head sat, impossible
crown at the small of her back.
Serpentine sisters, one could not
twist through the darkness without
shadow and echo, without the impossible
remembrance of the other
just as contorted,
held by the darkness, by sinister music
surrounded
by eyes puzzling
how humans could so bend.

A train of feathers trailed behind each
small girl, as they flew in
on smiles painted to shout
in the darkness
the silence of years of training.
They were perfect as swans, their pelvic bones
rising from the writhing of the
snakes within them, perfect
as we were.
Each of our legs could have belonged to the other
echoing our march into love,
the pale veins
tangling our blood, beating beneath
our skin, beyond history, beyond
the times still shocked
at how alike we were.

We bent, impossible twins, frantic wings
settling in the calm air of the room
at the center
of the circus of sun
and of darkness. We twisted
on the raised stage under the heartlight,
in the hidden tent
we lived.

We breathed
air of the other's breath,
we drank word and nectar of the other's dream,
we lived, impossible
in the hidden tent, slithered down
stairs, through the tympany of autumn leaves
to the store by the park, then I lay
against the tree, and we climbed
within the beating of feathers
to impossible addresses at the top of the light.

We were carried off, each of us bent back to face
our own bodies always trembling.
There is no music by which we can undo
the severing of our dreams,
full of shadows and wings.
There is no strong man
in animal skins and headdress of mail
to pick us up, one in each hand, and carry us,
feathers trailing, from the circus of sunlight
to the darkness
in the back of the tent.
Only our painted smiles, impossible twins,
remain.

ii. *The Strong Man*

You saunter to centerstage on grand haunches.
Ten gleaming weights ring out
their strength
as your assistants swing them
to the fragile floor.
You thread them, thin rod through
each hungry, surprised, bronze mouth.

You lift everything at once,
something I could
never do,
I who have been lifted
high above the sad dance,
willing, gasping, held up
by the line through the still
singing heart,

feet pointing to the fragile earth,
know that the strong man
is immeasureably stronger than I.

You lift us up,
high into dazzling space.
We burst, our heads pounding with music
of orbit and spinning through
the scattered dreams of all beings,
you lift
everything at once
for that instant
before you must
put us down on earth,
ringing with the weight of gravity grown
a millionfold with how high we've flown.

The weight of love is crushing
when the strong man sets it down.

iii.   *Clown Trotting in His Horse Costume*

One clown was his own horse, rising
above the toothy equine grin,
like a soul over the joke of its days.
Pretending to reign the gallop in,
he circled himself, encircled by horse,
each hoofbeat the ringing work of the invisible
master of sounds, each hoofbeat
setting the soul of the clown
spinning
within the blur of the scaffold of horse
round his hips, each hoofbeat
sending him closer to the edge
of the stage, the end
of his scene, until not even that sound
remained
as he followed himself
up the hill of the stage
to the room where his voice
sat quietly waiting.

iv.   Lady in White

caged in white you sing
your voice all the stronger
for how your costume holds you

you teach me
it is not our cell that measures voice
but the tent of the world we sing into

"They are there, their song is there"

The moon is in a glass bottle
on my windowsill, I dream
about my students all night.
I hear them shaking off chains.
Officials interrogate me about them,
call them wolves, statistics, criminals.
I try to tell the truth
but I am left with paintings of sand,
feathers settling to earth,
maps incised in the scalp,
photographs of children
being spat at or shot at.
I tell my secrets to my students,
they understand what my professors did not.
Trial by fire burns their lids off,
they look at me until they must turn away.

The one with bright eyes must have come from a star
one has a child kicking at the wall of her womb
one's eyes need me and he sobs as he pushes me away
one knows the histories but cannot repeat them
one adds up her family and never gets the right answer
this one waits by the locked door for the mother who has run away
that one sleeps with the breathing of strangers
many cry out in anger
many give gifts
each one labors to bring forth
runs from the hand at the throat or faces it and is cut
faces it and bleeds
long brilliant tracks follow behind.

I run after,
shouting whispering or singing.
I can never tell it
at the university or office,
but in the middle of long nights,
in my dreams of the carnival,
the breathless meals of lips and flesh,
the chase and the final death,

the prophecies that plague me,
they are there, their song is there.
In my empty palms
they twist around my lifeline, my heartline,
through the numbers of my marriages and children,
and in the dry empty space where my pulse beats,
volcanic, under threats of fire, flood, avalanche
and ferocious winds that keep the earth turning.

IMMIGRANTS

Brixton Photo

A man with one eye winks at me.
He lost the other in a brawl:
white men swinging, wood to his head.
A splinter entered his sight, rain fell softly,
and his mother, about to cry out,
dropped the paper sack
from her arms.

Now he leans over the fence, his spine
is bent, breath comes hard. *This*, he says,
is what we were invited to London for,
and those who serve
for a bit of bread
take notice.

Without this fence to lean on, this mother
with empty arms, he might wander the earth
in search of a cliff high enough to fling himself from
and fly without crashing
before he loses breath.

In this way I wander the earth, one-eyed,
blinded, third-eyed, an ocean
of visions flooding me
so that even with my eyes closed,
even in the twilight of deep winter or power failure,
entombed alive in the cruelty
of this current turning,
I can see without end
the swirling of skirts of many colors,
the insides of mouths, teeth flashing
and the soft rain of gums and tongues;
I see the weapons that rip open the night,
children fallen to the bloodthirst of parents,
creatures with many legs passing over my face and body,
the phallus above me and inside me, yes, I can see
even this with my eyes that rove and burrow
and fly in the fine weathers,
weep and sparkle in the rains and mists.

Trevor with his empty eyelid has told the police
his story. They have written a report
but his other eye sees them toss it
into the trash around the corner.
He dreams of a golden orb with the blackest center
journeying through the night to enter him,
fill out his puckered face,
and change forever the face of what he sees.

Burning

Each night my grandfather wandered through the unraveling bobbins, tossing the grays, caressing the crimsons, and begged us to stop blocking the light so he could bend to the cloth of his sister and stitch her and stitch her. He raised a glass of schnapps to put out, he said, her flaming hair. He raced around the room to catch a doll floating through the bare limbs of March, and wrapped her in his prayers, little sister's name sewn through the blanket of Hebrew. We caught him as he leaned from the cool stone sill of tenement. He was holding on, he wept, to the burning soles of her feet, swaying like a ship, hair crackling at the bolted door.

He gathered the leaves of fall into envelopes and printed names on their tongues. He walked into night to search, his note said, for coins from the old pay envelope scattered when his sister flew. We found him worshipping the sky from the steerage of trashcans in downtown alleys, wrapping himself in distant languages. We led him home to sit at his sewing machine. He smashed the lightbulbs, shouting fire! and tried to douse the sun with buckets of mopwater. He wore three wool jackets even in summer, though he burned with it, he burned.

Empty factory windows opened in his eyes when his granddaughter screamed, her hand at the stove so close her wings could catch, he whispered, holding her, crushing the embers he said could devour her.

They told us children not to run from him, but we cried that he smelled of smoke. We know that he swallowed himself, choking dry, water saved in buckets by the bed. We remember how long he lay under the blanket before he shouted that it could fly and he with it. His fingers still burn our faces.

Immigrants

i. Looking for the Angel

I can't remember, I was trying to go home.
The laughter was too loud, the wind was picking up.
I had long rips, like scars from surgery, down my stockings.
The laughter swooped over my shoulder on a fast bike,
erupted from an old car, pulling me in,
into darkness of sand from night beaches,
darkness spilling from broken bottles,
darkness of airless fumbling,
breath without air, without voice.
Only the man's breath, only his stubs of fingers,
only his judgment,
only the night where I cannot walk.

If I found the street, I lost the apartment,
then the room, then the face.
After never sleeping in the same bed twice,
the waves washed over me
filling my emptiness
with salt water and the driven particles
of sand.

Now I am staying put.
The air flies about, landing like small birds
in my lungs.
I move close to him to inhale that breath of life
he doesn't know is fragrant.
I take what he holds out to me.

ii. Story

There is a story we can't forget.
There is a vigil we keep for each flame,
each desecrated street, each windy hallway,
each impossible room buried
under things moved in from elsewhere,
each child torn from us, a vigil
for the perfect back of the one we want
to stay with.

We know the death of the clock
in the endless embrace, we hold
the man or the woman against us
in great disbelief, seized
by the shock of beauty
in the breath of the one
we want to stay with,
as in all we would remain with,
talking on the corner,
joking in the market,
striding next to each other
with our voices and our warm hands.

iii.   Change

The streets repeat themselves
with machine guns, arrests,
the chance that everything will change.
There will be shoes and bread
and doctors and schools,
but on the black slate is written
the question of the fearful
and of the ones in love
for the last time,
"How many will die first?"

iv.   Immigrants

I return each night to the one I want to stay with.
He returns each night to his country.
Sometimes I'm there, sometimes not,
and sometimes I'm back on the boat,
pushed to the rail,
face pale as an old sea,
watching the shoreline recede,
counting the countries
of quotas already met,
deportations for speaking up,
raids and the emptied factories,
lines of the new foreign-born,
their English grateful and deceived.

I might make it,
I might find a country to take me in.
I might find a language to keep on speaking
until I die, I might
hold the one I want to stay with
so close I can smell his country,
the air might nest in my lungs,
fly from branch to branch of the same tree,
sing in my homebound throat,
blow gently over my long body,
over the back and the belly
of the one I want
to stay with,
the bare dreams, the paired breaths,
sand falling from our fingers,
darkness held down beneath us.

Everything will change though we stay,
everything will remain though darkness fill us.

v.   Return

The angel has gone home,
taken his breath that turns the earth.
My breath stops at the end of the world,
I see the small boat going over the edge,
I blink until I can see the angel
eating dinner out of a plastic container,
leaning back from a corner of the kitchen table.
Birds sing to him, dogs are calmed and listen,
shining their eyes in the direction of his cloud of hair.
He looks at the food, he looks up,
he is not sure where to look.
All day he has read newspapers,
looked at many faces,
watched subway stops streak past him,
watched women's backs and ignored their eyes.
All day long he has turned history over in his hands,
run with it zipped into his thin jacket.

In 1965 he knew where Vietnam was.
He knew it was the other side of the earth,
the other side of his own country.
He said so, with others, in the streets.

If this angel doesn't come back,
listen, there are others,
there is no limit, as precious as this angel be,
many will rise in his place

but here, in this moment,
in this room and bed filled with dreams,
the scent of history on the run lingers,
the impression of an exhausted body in the mattress
remains
although the clouds fly high off
the pillow and the wood floor,
although tonight he sleeps on a sofa
in front of a silent television,
although the light of false histories
shines from the screen
onto his cheek and forehead,
although my blood rises, an ocean in a storm,
and the day which has turned away from us
will turn back
into the clocks we set, the dry bread we nibble,
the letters which have fallen
from the angel's hand
and been swept away.

In the night, the hands of the angel
are set like the clock,
one at rest on the heart
and the other, empty,
dangling over the side of the sofa,
adrift in the darkness.

What the angel dreams is forgotten
when the day turns back.
He says he dreams only about strangers,
but there is a stranger who watches
the impression of his body
slowly rise up from her bed
and step from the apartment.
There is a stranger who turns toward him
many times a day,
there is a sound she makes that is not singing,
but neither is it a cry,
a sound which the angel cannot understand
when his face turns away from her in flight

from one island to another
and all he wants is to return
to the only heaven he knows,
though he find it without milk, without sweetness.

vi.   *Counting*

The years fall into my back,
that sad arc, half circle of fear,
that clinging to fences.
Years fall into my eyes
carrying a vision through cruel wires
of someone else's history.
Through the years histories are exchanged
as if I shook the dry rattle
from every bed and hammock,
floors of dirt, walls of paper,
green fields and scorched earth.
Dumb heart, before language,
pushes against its ribs,
finds words, writes letters
no guard will deliver,
feet meet each other
in their search for resemblance,
anything in pairs a miracle to the eyes
that stare off in opposite directions
or rest, at opposite hours,
sharing the head
as poor immigrant workers their cots.

Years fall into my hands, into the thin, veined skin.
So many years turn the pages of newspapers,
so many invasions they must be put on microfilm,
the thousands of tiny Marines
visible only to the eyes that hunt for them.
I hold a small light to each face
which repeats the eyes till the light goes out.
These troops measure the years
as do the shouts of the invaded
and the hurled rocks and heavy guns
in the hands of fifteen-year-olds
who rise against them,

so many years fall into the blood of these children
that their blood, unfurled
from the star of blood at their foreheads,
brings blindness to one eye
and the clearest vision to the other.

So many years in my aching teeth I must bite,
women draped in furs beware.
Men hailing cabs, with leather cases
filled with death, beware,
so many years in my aching teeth I must bite.
So many photos of his years since April,
so many years since the invasion of one country,
so many invasions since the month of April.
We watch the flour wasted from the sack,
our hands grip the wounds in the cloth.
Children without shoes
learn to do their arithmetic in this way:
counting Aprils, counting Marines,
bringing with them each smaller child.

vii. Flight

Beyond the window
the angel is flying wildly over the map,
crossing the bluest waters stained with blood.
He tries to hold too much in his wings,
sometimes they are empty.
The angel is sorry and hurts like a man,
his face is shattering.
The woman on the ground feels
she is shattering, too.
She has thrown many books into the waters, many papers,
she has closed her eyes
to let the angel whirl through the dark room
rather than finish her story in the old way,
one separate woman speaking in the night.
She has shut the light and settled into bed
with the angel's face and hands and cloud of hair,
his smell like a man
and his thousands of miles.
She wants to push his letters out of bed.
She wants to travel with him.
She can. She has learned.

The angel does not understand where he is
and writes so many letters home.
Someone lives there and reads them
and kisses the angel when she can.
He takes those kisses in
and comes back to finish his passion,
but he flies about her thin shoulders, stares at her,
and then, sadly, a man who sometimes has nothing,
covers his head with one wing
and wraps the other around her.

The angel knows he is wrong and can never be right.
The woman has been the angel for someone else.
They both fell in a world
where there is more than one country on the map,
more than one woman's face,
more than one man's.
They are both tired
of gathering faces that shatter
and so he flies wildly
over her house, then over the map
to a heaven in flames, to a country in revolt,
to a woman of the same blood,
and the other, the woman on the ground,
holds the angel's face in her eyes
and looks into the long years
she had so often counted
like precious beads on a child's necklace
or sweets that must last,
and sees only the tasks,
her hands moving on the slow-moving line,
the time like a long absence,
and the angel flying in and out of her room,
her sky, her exhausted dreams.

viii.   History

The angel has come back from his country.
For the first time
he looks older, his laugh is smaller.
He reaches for children he can play with,
they turn away.

There is a *baile*.
The women still dance with him
but they all go home to their lovers,
or their husbands and children.

She is there, too. Why
not, she goes
in black, *como una viuda*.
She dances
in her way, he dances
with her, her hair flies, she is warm in her stomach,
she can remember.
History is not only that of whole peoples,
it is also the story of each light,
what is behind the face
momentarily turned away from the world.

As he dances with her, the angel looks beyond.
She thinks this is the only way
he can look straight at her,
but still
she begins to disappear.

At the door he smiles.
They hold out their hands and touch fingertips
for an instant, then, as if burned,
pull away.
The angel, like a man,
pushes her into the street with her friends,
watches them walk away, then stares
up the steps to the dark apartment.
Looking back she sees him pushing the glass door,
entering and disappearing.

His reflection, being an angel's,
remains in the glass he is constantly entering,
so it is the image of himself he walks into,
the darkness holding up the glass,
the silence behind the door.

Now she puts her hands together
to crush something she has been holding
into the broken circle of her palms.

THE STREET OF THE LOST CHILD

The Street of the Lost Child

What in our lives could possibly be a poem?
What could grow soft enough to fit into words?
Who would read them,
who would read your life—
    the ones who laughed at it
    or those who struck it, over and over,
    with pleasure or efficiency?
who will care that you almost died,
that others did,
that you cannot stop weeping
and your laughter is the most delicate thing you have?
Who will care
that children you were, children you touched,
are silent and lost,
or that there is a street in another city
you cannot leave
though you wander down the wide avenues
tossed from north to south,
a siren always in your throat,
wanting only to lie down
and fit your bones into those of another,
one who has found your street,
who can warm your throat, coaxing the laughter out of it,
who can teach you to sleep, teach you to close your eyes
and sleep, turn off the avenue and enter him
until his empty hands open and are filled with you.

This is not what was whispered to you
on the *Calle del Niño Perdido.*
You were a girl, pushed to the wall
or down into the damp carseat before daylight.
You had to open or remain closed forever, they said,
open your mouth, we will fill it, they said,
open your legs and we will fill you.
They did not say that your tongue could dance,
that you could take a man,
you could get up and speak
above him, into him,
without him.

Calle del Niño Perdido—Street of the Lost Child, in Mexico City

Elegy

We are lying together
and you are the one who is searching inside me,
you are the one I am eating and drinking,
the one whose hands hold me up,
whose breath keeps me alive,
whose body works against me until it loses its fury,
whose throat lies in honey,
whose limbs are sculpted in the journey,
whose aching forehead falls into song only once
or twice, then into fever,
then into the ancient cave of shadow.

You become the one who does not know me,
who could not wait for blossom.
This was the love whose elegy
I will sing until I die,
this was the transformation into history
of the demon night.
Here was the acrid smoke
the fan gently turning
through the days and nights
could not dispel.
This is what won't release me:
the hours in your arms,
watching your body move toward me
through the long hall of the railroad apartment,
watching your body move away,
your sad silent ear,
your dim lost eye,
your perfect skin and the caught tongue,
the dance we never did,
your memories, mine,
and the sad grandfather smoking cigarettes all day long
at the raised window across the airshaft,
one child crying at his feet
tormented by another.

Paraplegia

i.   O, the people I've met
as I loll in my chair.
I'm the girl of the golden wheel.
Spin me.

ii.   The dancing
has never stopped.
Can you
hear me
whirling?

iii.   No one will ever
watch me as I walk,
though ride through the streets
I will,
going home
to the body of dreams.

iv.   I raised my eyes, my neck
is weak but the sun
came up and exploded
its song, fell through the waves
of the cold gray sky
and I felt heat
in my thighs,
I felt heat.

v.   No one knows
how light this steel
can be,
how leaden.

vi.   My name rolls away
beneath me.
It rides high
to the top of the wheel
and is crushed.
Fortune sings over it,
and the name of a man
I will never meet again
rumbles alongside
a foot away,

leaves its imprint
in the snow.

vii. No other cage for this tiger,
a rolling grave,
a daily war,
a room with a view,
the world wrapped in beauty
before me,
unopened.

viii. Shh, sweet girl, sleep,
I tell myself.
Tomorrow we'll go for a walk,
tomorrow.

ix. I'm exhausted. I've beaten
my arms against the sides
of the chair, they are bruised blue
and death has not come.
No one has called me home,
no one waits across the street
for me to race
into their arms.
No one knows
how quickly I would come.
No one knows
the sweetness of my arms.

x. What would you have done,
trapped here?
Some do more, some
less.
Rings, rivers, rockets,
all shine in my chair,
a silver blues
hurtling
through the corner
of your eye,
faster
than you can know me,
bless me
or undo me.
I'm going home
to the body of dreams.

River Lament for Those Who Knew Derek

River of trucks, the stuck cars,
needles of bikes and gallop of hearse
over the Hudson. The hanged boy
swings from the Bridge, the Washing-
ton Bridge, as echoes of foghorn
fall into the throat
of the river.

Sounds of the boy weeping in his cell
float in the river's ears, its cups of light.
The rope uncoils as the river
passes beyond the city
and the beaten piers
disappear
into heavy grasses
that sway at the river's edge,
brush against its journey
and hush the boy's crying.

We want a river of trumpets,
the swan calling out before he was clubbed,
the rush of river back before rope,
before club, before river was sorrow
that wound through our intestines,
when what glittered was light, the flash of fish
and birds flying, calling, mating, within view
of the river rush, the suspended bridge
that could hold us.

We remember the singing river,
the shuddering bridge,
the sky, empty, that opened
to the north,
when we could hear
the swan lift his neck,
when we couldn't hear
the club come down.

Notes on a Phone Call

Snow piles up, crouched outside
the silent window. Sharto, skinny with deaths,
calls from Brooklyn, his bent back an echo of my own,
his "too many" words like Amadeus' notes
in the movie he gazes at as we speak.
Child of Langston at seven, child of loss at fifteen,
death by bullet, she dies in his arms,
his hope escaping from her lips,
her words wrapped around his heart.

Sharto's a rhyming king of the nineties
metaphysical poets, alchemist of my classroom.
Grand Ebony eyes him,
talks him up, calls him late,
but he's heartdriven by the girl he would marry.
Sharto, another brilliant one,
his voice deeper than my decades past,
gets into the SAT class, college-bound, heading on.
He'll leave Brooklyn and study
in the deep ice night of Binghampton.

But Otis sings, Otis drives his heart home
to my memory: that day Sharto comes in and
sits silent, till he tells us it's a repeat.
The girl he loves at nineteen just hit-and-run,
she lives all weekend in the hospital
at the end of the crash, she dies
in his hands. He comes to my class
and sits at the computer, silent,
stares at the snow on the screen
whirling through the ice of late spring,
and wraps words around his heart, torn and still so tender.
Dear Sharto, old soul, beam of light
in the whirling New England winter
so far from Brooklyn, from my classroom,
from the one I was.

When We Can't Speak

When we can't speak
when the clock has wound down
and the flowers begin to fall apart
gently, as if that flight
were all their lives,
we must find the child's toy,
the tiny house made of wood
with its ridiculous turrets
and staircases, its blind
windows, and we must enter,
each thin stick of us,
and look out from the archway
past the dull knife that shaped
the architecture we are caught in.

In the hospital
before and after he died
it was the hands, once
enormous with the difference
in our ages, then swollen past
my adult hands
with the fluids of the end
accumulating, then falling,
leaving the body
a parched field
where the rain flees.

Each time the husband's smile turns
wrong, we see the father,
each time the word withheld,
the face come stone,
the hand opens and drops us out.
Each time he clothes his soul
and his eyes pull back,
we fall through
and the old cyst breaks and poisons.

We who have gone with our father and our mother,
we who have never lain with anyone,
we who must take death pure
as it comes, here
in our schoolclothes,
dark skirts over our knees,
when do we begin to live?
We wait for three o'clock,
for summer vacation,
we tiptoe around the cup's edge,
never fully see our reflection
nor the one looking over our shoulder,
we must not drink, we wait
against the cold wall,
the dance goes on forever
without us.

In the ancient circle death
holds his hand, I can
no longer.
I kneaded the fingers
and the disturbing hills,
the unfulfilled whorls
on the shrinking fingertips,
I pounded on the river of pulse
but only his eyes danced
in convulsion, and this storm
held no promises, no soft whispers
for me, merely the dizzying sight
of a man begging
to be flung over the edge,
looking without hope to every corner,
until the room, so carefully set,
came down all around him.

We who have gone with our father and our mother,
ignorant of the blood and why it flows,
have grown monstrous
while the woman inside us
has learned of the blood
and lain down, eyes to the ceiling,
to begin.

Again and again they reach for us,
and in the reflected beginning
of our love away from them,
the sad echo thuds against the wall
of our heart, and the dark skirt
must be ripped away.

Only when the face we wake to
becomes entirely new, can we see it
in all its wondrous light,
and the field dances with us
and the flowers know their spring.

Mother Is Carried Off

Mother is carried off in a white nightgown,
legs and back so bent we worry
she will not fit inside her skeleton's last home.
Mother is carried off into light of those dead
before her, she chanted their names to
block mine out, me alive, too large, too loud,
me believing
she was my mother.
No one remembered my birth, all were drugged
with fear.
No one laid a hand on my hair
without wrenching snakes from their bone home.
No one celebrated the stretching of my body
into girl, then into woman, all was too much,
too loud, the groaning
of the bones beaten back,
each inch of cloth resented
as if mother's father at his machine
was locked to the treadle for my sake.

Mother is carried off
in a white nightgown, cigarette smoke and lysol
in the air today, her pretty cheekbones jutting
out from her motionless face, eyecups
sunken but the swirl of grey hair
a softer gift than she ever granted
during those years of scrubbing us like bad pots,
no one believing
her fury, her brutal turning
of our skin to raw fear,
to the other side of the planet,
to the cringing of what is beaten
and what is scraped raw.

No one sees her hands now. They are buried
in the folds
of the robe she never wore alive.
They are glowing hot
in the new satin, in their old rages,
they are larger than anyone can see,

and what is buried in the folds of my skin,
tanned and older than my imagination
could foresee, is howling, alone in ceremony,
alone in the gracious sunlight of October,
alone with the bones
of my mother and my waiting father,
and people wonder
where I've gone and I can't tell them
because the words for this are those of a child

and I've run away,
used my tongue to tell another story,
but still I want those words,
those little first words,
to tell this story,
to be believed.

THESE SNAPSHOTS I HAVE LOST

"The woman seated made a sign of death"

"Shortly after a cease-fire was signed yesterday, a group of Croatian
women gathered in the streets of the Bosnian town of Novi Travnik
to halt a Muslim civilian convoy carrying food to Tuzla. Croatian
forces then attacked the stalled convoy. The woman seated made
a sign of death."—*The New York Times*, June 11, 1993

No one can tell you
what flowers
from the hearts
of the other tribe.
Seated as stone, your lance
a wooden plank, your scarf
tied at the back of your neck,
old flowered dress pulling
open at the belly
while the other tribe starves,
bone embraces bone as they wait
for the trucks of food
you and your old sisters stop.
Your men are no longer men,
but soldiers.
You wink, your finger slashing
across the throat, sign of death,
blood pact with the boots and the eyeless,
the uniforms that hover over the dreams
of raped Muslim women as dead skin, cold,
that sleeps afterwards without dreaming.
Finger travels your own fat throat, glutted now on blood,
more fed, more need for it,
as you make a sign of death ringed by your sisters
and halt the convoy of trucks that tries to make its way
to Muslim Tuzla, carrying food
as you once did to your own children,
housewives now, and workers.

How have you decided this, how do you know
with the absolute solidity of your seated body,
your wide lined face, eyes half closed,

that you must do as you do, stop the food, invite the soldiers
to kill those traveling in trucks
with sacks of flour, canned milk, potatoes?
Some try to argue with you. You sit, certainty roaring
in your finger.

Starvation comes for Tuzla under the sign of death:
the angry, heartless sister
her finger traveling through time
across her throat until, satisfied
with its journey into the air
beside her, it falls to her lap
as if she is an old lady, weak
and without tricks, but the air
vibrates with her slashing, the air
has been cut and turns to flee
the cries that follow
in the airless shaft of hunger,
the devouring gasp of rape.

The woman who makes the sign of death
has not gotten up from her chair all afternoon.
Beg her to raise herself up so that you may see
her ankles, the worn leather of her shoes, so you may know
she has walked in the dust of towns, seen others' hungers.
But her mouth will not move. Her body will stay crouched and full
on the wooden throne. Her finger will rise up.

Her dress is old. Who would do as she tells them?
Not her own sons.

They have married Muslim girls.

These Snapshots I Have Lost
1987

When somehow the burning of the sun,
its sacrifice of wings,
its circle of burning, of abandoning
the half of us
and illuminating to skeleton
the rest of us, fearful
in the light, yet exultant
in our hair of ash,
when this flame, unnoticed, entered
the dim interior of my camera,
all the colors of that July in Moscow
bled into the dark pool of the past.
The translucent wings of swan
rising from the lake at Gorky Park
were towed under,
the kopecks hit the lake's center
and fell straight to the middle
of the hidden earthen pot,
and each witness to war
stepped behind a birch or a pine
and was taken by shadow.

These snapshots join the hook of film
screeching on the brittle spine
bent to me since I first sought
air or milk or the glowing
face framed by my blurred vision
and my hungers; what I sought gasping
was only what I would lose,
and each locked bedroom door
could not keep it from being so.

Lost are all the days
echoing in the wind in my hand,
the days of childhood widening
till they reached their night and then,
exhausted, fled;
and those nights that howled
in the cries from the other room,
in the open shuddering cup of bone,
in my small body that grew and lifted off the bed
and fought to pass through the window,
always broken,

into the cleft of air from where
no hands could pull me back,
but the voices took me,
and the hands made me over
into a woman,
into a worker, into a name
and an age.

Now all the silent frames spinning
on their shadow spine
must bleed into the light:
father   mother   sister   bed
knife   pants   window
floor   dreams
and the journeys of nighttime,
its stirrings and silence,
the door slamming
and something closing in my heart.
Hands over my mouth
and at my neck, hands
and all that I was held in them:

all of the flesh and the young limbs
and the bursting star inside,
the heavy swaying of the waters around me,
the new moon cutting my sight,
the anger of trees, the anger
of the large hands that feared my body,
the shattering of the glass as it slipped
away from me,
the endless spilling of milk
onto the mopped floor, the flowing
of its pale sickness, my mother's
collapse into spinning,
coils of my hair left
in her bitter fingers.
And all that was seen was eyeless,
all that was face could not be touched,
all that was hand was single-shadowed,
and foot cried, and cells swarmed with fear.

And all that was film lived there, only,
stacked in the dusty boxes,
face after face of laughing photos,
but I knew black coil behind them,

I knew
box of darkness, pinpoint of light,
hard fall of the shutter,
opposite eye recoiling from the light
and slow chemicals that eat at us,
give us face after face
like cars through the window,
their stark lights in procession:
sirens spinning through, tires
against the pitted road, the angry curve,
thrown against each other, sister
against sister, wife
against husband,
shocked, cries, then moving again
to the four corners of the gray Ford,
four winds circling the heart.

And now this new journey
sinks behind the silent film that refused
all light and color, all form and face,
wanders off into the dim world
of last summer, the past world left
on the other side of spinning.

With this film burned black by silent sun
I have lost
the town of my father's birth, his reasons
for leaving,
all that my grandparents said and knew
before they reached the silence and forgetting
of the new land, I have lost
the domed church before which we were ridiculed,
the hand at my shoulder,
the shadows of buildings,
many eyes and many children,
the shouts of the crowd where Lenin spoke,
his words and theirs,
everything that shone and suffered
from the corner of the room where Pushkin wrote,
where Chekhov wrote,
the bread and the cheese that finally fell to the ground
in abundance, the crows
demanding my flesh,
the block where the poor man was beheaded,
the square where his cries rang out,
many pairs of shoes in the store window on Kallinin

as in the death camp at Panerai,
where their owners were lost
in the hammering of bullets,
in the slow slow fires,
in the scattering of ash
by hands, by wind,
by the ringing beads of each moment.

I held the blackened film as if fire
had blazed up and burned to ash
all that I had gathered that July,
all that my people left behind when they fled,
all the shivering music they had spun with their bodies
and in the dreams that throbbed in the pinched skulls
of village winters, as the last fires
sputtered and went out
before all became motion,
before they took the land and the water
in a fever to arrive,
to sever the roots
of the giant tree they were carved from.

I wept as if the slow Moscow dawn were dead,
its colors buried, its songs silenced,
gone the dishes striking against each other's
gleaming hearts in the hotel kitchen,
gone the worker dressed in white
standing in the early shaft of sunlight
or the last rays of the moon,
while I stood behind the curtain
and watched in the lost night of all blackness
and all light, in my dream of earth,
of body upon body, sliding
into the summer rain.

Was it the sunlight that obliterated
the images of families in the parks and streets
of my wandering?
What hammer falling daily
smashed the most delicate part of the eye
that shone that summer, how can I return
to seeing? What stillness flooded
the pits at Panerai
where families lined up along the edge
for one instant

before their backward flight exploded
and the unwinding streamer of their last moment
tied them together?

I thought the faces of these true angels
were singing and glowing in the black canister of my film
as my passport was stamped in the dismal light of the last morning
and I passed through gate after gate,
released from the song of wind above the pits,
released from the moment when I too fly backwards,
all the bright and holy air above me,
all the naked women like myself
become soft mist
that shudders against the cold laughter of the shots
that do not ring out
because now there is only silence and light.

I was not there at the stark edge of the pit
but I spin off again and again
into the current of night that carries me there,
I lose my breath buried in the dim chest of sleep,
I claw at the hand that obliterates, without fatigue,
the lines of women and girls, and men and boys,
I am blinded by the light that flashed above their whispers.

And all about, their faces still fly
above ash, above water,
in the torrent and stillness,
in the silent rooms
and the drench of dreams,
in every hard and soft thing,
in every color,
in the velvet blackness beyond the birch,
in the devouring snow
that overtakes, blinds, freezes,
remembers nothing.

And all who waited in the still patterns of the walls,
beyond the garden, in the sad dust beneath the cart
of the vendor, in the threads of his remnants,
without land or a whole uncracked kettle,
all who bore the names of the old music
and even then spoke with the double tongue
of Russian and Yiddish
or of serf and man

or of property and woman,
all who spun about in the dance within
and knew the passing of carriages
and the long nights of the ballroom
lit to brilliance in the bitter January
or in the long bitter days of flower,
stepped back in the shadow
and seemed blind and dumb
to the rumors in the balcony
at Ostankino Palace, now the Palace
of Serf Art
where the story in the center of the dance floor
is woven into the rich fabric that wraps the white body,
is stitched to the death of the lamb at her feet,
swoons from the sweet clouds rising from the whales' agonies,
is painted delicately on the scroll of the serf,
and glides over the ballroom floor,
over the intricate wood inlay of simple peasants
who await the turning of the century
over and over
dizzy under the gliding step of the dancing czars,
almost blind in the storm of light unleashed
by the baroque candelabras
carved by the serfs as they slowly straightened.

On the last day caught within
the last frame of her own dying image,
the large woman in the white apron
is clicking her counter madly and grinning,
clicking us into the Pushkin
to stand and stare up at the unchanging David
whose beauty pulses in the lump of vein at his ankle,
as in mine

then the metro glides
through the city and faces
pass us without end on the escalator
that rumbles us off
hard onto our feet
just as each bead of the cashier's
abacus knocks hard against the one
before it, releases a sound
that, spinning, hits
the dying well water
and pronounces the cost of our living.

Questions of War

You are my chance to see myself naked in another's eyes,
to go beyond my bones to the dream that holds us up,
but the bones of so many others are being smashed
in this horrible repeat, repeat, rerun of Vietnam,
only this time no images come to the screen
of the country beneath the bombs.
This time all is surgical, Baghdad is
a hotel room with two or three frightened voices
whispering in Standard American English
what they hear through the floor,
what they see through the window.
There is no tall uniform blowing the brains out
of a thin Vietnamese peasant
who kneels on the screen until he flies away
from the bursting stream of his brains,
there is no screaming mother running
with her burnt and burning child in her arms
away from the village
which is renamed napalm.

Reporting, like the bombing,
is surgical, and I am dying
to be in love
in this second half of my life.
We sit by the TV holding each other,
grim face next to grim face,
old angers surrounding our hearts,
but inside them
the warmth of crossed and tangled limbs,
the searching of hands and tongues,
the deep rocking seas.

Our "patriots" know as much about Iraq as they knew
about Vietnam,
and in Baghdad, in Basarah, the sky is falling.
"What a beautiful sight!" someone sighs.

Some pilot in Norfolk, Virginia,
who spent his Friday nights drinking
and trying to "lay some girl"
is painting messages to Saddam Hussein
on the side of the bomb his plane will deliver,
and that night some girl in Iraq
will feel her spirit fly out from her
and her sad body weep over itself,
over the shattering of symmetry
of limbs, eyes, breasts.

"Our boys,"
but only in war.
The beautiful young ones, beautiful to me,
throwaways to this country—
now they wrap them up in yellow ribbons
and give them away to the worst hungers.
"I do not want to write this poem"
—I heard this line in another's poem
from one of the last wars
or one of the last murders
of one of the young black men, sweet and fierce,
who didn't last long enough to be one of "our boys"
—maybe he was painting graffiti,
maybe he was going to buy a used car,
maybe he whistled at the wrong woman,
I do not want to write this poem.

But always twisting this globe of darkness
in my old hands, I see the other side
of the planet in darkness and I wonder
what dead name the soldiers will learn
to give the Iraqis.
We know there is always an other,
we know we would rather not be the other,
we know there are Arabs who own groceries,
Arabs who don't speak English,
Arabs who might be terrorists.
We know the news is censored but believe
for terrible long moments
the sorting of the hacked pieces
into "us" and "them."
I can't
march along.

I am dizzy on the fleeing circle of earth.
I want to pray to all the gods.
I'll try the anguish of the hidden cross
and the trampled star and burning crescent.
I will learn Iraq's old gods,
Inanna of Khafajah, also named
Ishtar, cause and mother of the world,
the air-god Enlil of Nippur,
the moon-god Nannar of Ur,
and the water-god Enki, goat and fish,
who wants to preside over our cleansing by water,
not by fire and blood.
I'll kneel before the blazing altar and the black
and white chickens who eat and are eaten,
and the rattle filled with vertebrae of snake
that shakes my heart with it
until I can see the mirror of the universe all around me
but especially in your eyes, in your hands,
in your gracious limbs that cover us both.

There is a drum beating in the cave inside me
there is a great tree on the hill outside
there are two smaller trees which flank it
and through them I enter.
I hover there and to anyone who passes,
I say, "This is my church.
I am praying for the war to end."

But is this the cleansing,
is this what was promised and feared?
Has it been coming for a long time?
Is this the earth shaking us off?
Is this the air raid siren
that will catch me far away from you?
Will my prayer be your name
as "their boys,"
who would love my smile and my desert bones,
break off our romance with their own missiles,
leave my students' papers uncorrected
and strangely silent, show the worst fears
of my tortured mother as reality?

Will I fly through the empty hiss of air
and see you looking up and searching the light,
will you fly to me,
can we stop this war?
Will they tell us how many are dead per tax dollar?
Is it just the way it is, must I give in?
Can I dream our way out of this?
Can I make the hands of war tremble
with their burden of blood?
Will the sand that covers
the bones of my ancestors
cover us all? Will I find you,
can we bear it,
will our child be healed?

From September 11: "By 1740, one in every six
New Yorkers was owned by another New Yorker"
—from *New York: A Documentary Film*, written and directed
by Ric Burns

i.   *The Fall*

No
she said, and she
fell, as the great hands of the
blast pushed her
beyond falling, pushed her
from the sound of her daily
life, pushed from office, from xerox,
though to either side of her
the fall was duplicated, pushed her
from desk and chair,
her last sitting, pushed her
from telephone, from call
waiting, and many
would wait on the other end
for months, for word, for body,
which she had left some time during
the fall.

　　　The blast pushed her to
do the one thing she'd always had
trouble doing—yell the one word
nobody listened to
when she'd whisper it, over and
over, no, to the insistent hands.
Then,
　　　　　No!
　　　　　she called out as she fell, and
　　　　　next to her fell a man who had often
　　　　　heard that word whispered, and with pleasure
　　　　　pushed aside the small trembling
　　　　　letters.

         No, he cried out finally
to the violence of others,
but all we heard, watching, as we often do,
was the loud blast and its
heavy, deafening power,
the wind of its invisible hands,
and the small frightened sound
of our own voices, saying, No,

this isn't happening.

ii.   The Climb

And each morning, it was like this—jolting over the Bridge from
Brooklyn, where the subway rises into the air between the buildings,
over the sea, with the common breath in and the exhalation of dreams
joined to the sea air that moves through the car, as he held on to strap
and pole, jousted for footing with each lurch, drifted back to dreaming,
heavy under the eyelids

He was journeying from his neighborhood and its brilliant music of
Creole, its symphony of islands, Haiti, Trinidad, Barbados, Jamaica, oh
man he was traveling in his mind back to breadfruit and sorrel, not
knowing why it was so strong this morning—the fragrance, the ocean
breeze, Mama's scolding as he climbed the giving trunk of the palm and
laughed down at her

Proud, she was, as he climbed like a grown man, but afraid for him.
What you think, she shouted up at him, your head's a coconut? What if
you fall? But he didn't. He came down slow and perfect to show her he
was safe, and she hugged him. He'd stay safe for her, he told her then,
because she was his best girl. He told her this

Again at the airport the day he left for New York, this hard place.
Trouble plenty there, she said, you better watch yourself. And he did,
lord, he did, and went to work and school, and came home to his
cousin's living room sofa to dream about someday. He'd get a place and
bring Mama here, and she'd watch him climb up into the sky, above
the canopy of trees

Beyond where she could see him to scold, in a great office building that
shadowed itself into the heavens. He'd climb, after security waved him
through, by trembling elevator, for early shift, and push the cart with its

grand piles of mail—he knew each name and each office and desk— as
he walked by windows high above the glittering, dirty streets, the dark,
murmuring waters

If Mama could see him, she'd know he'd be safe. A good boy, you are,
she told him the day he left. Just remember. Your head, it's not no
coconut. Be careful when you climbing trees

iii.   The Burial

This rage will take you down, she tells herself, but she can't help it,
as she weaves down the street, as she screams, short and bitter spurts of
rage, hungry
above the hard trod of old shoes,
cast off.
This day she has cleaned up and will sit, without too many stares,
in the underground cafe at Borders,
she who is crossing,
she who can read, though she has nothing to eat,
she whose voice is softer than the edge of her,
the sharp edge that will cut you if you come close.

She has fine skin, that ash will cover.
She has long stride, that explosion will break.
She has wild hair, that will sizzle with angels.
She has dreams, that will become rain.
She has fingers, that will stop counting.
She has eyes, that open in the country of books.
She has song
that slips out in public, becomes prayer
in the smallest beat of time.

She will live forever in the in-between, in the other light
you keep her in, in the waters aching to cover, in the shadow
of the wall become a street, in the first thefts
that began wealth in the new world,
in the rage that will melt her down to bone.

She will disappear
into the one address
she never would have claimed, the grand
accusation of towers
over invisible tribes at the base of the island.

Her step will finish, but will live in the way stone
smashes against more stone, as when Africans built the wall
in the way that slaves must build.

She'll haunt the sidewalk where the wall was taken down
to make business of the earth, make street of blossom.

No one will look for her.

With no address, she lies above the final body count.
She is not alone. There are many, singing and raging.
She is not bare bones, pure ash, unreadable absence.
Someone has written his rage all over her.
Does the smoke of her tell his story?
It does not tell hers.

Easter Heart

Oh what can you tell me this Easter Sunday, neighbors,
what can you tell my dismal heart?
What can you say this Easter
to the one who wept for hours the last time
the Sunday rain beat down on the earth
and flooded the souls who strained to come back
to those they had left behind?
My eyes leap in their sockets and cannot rest
when they see you always under the ax
or walking innocently the great earth
that is mined with hatred,
or lifting your sleek heads
to meet the bullet's ancient trajectory
or slowly falling into your graves
because the thin gruel cannot sustain you.
Can you show me the blossom death is,
can you show me the heart of the world?
Illuminate my mourning room
that is strewn with newspapers and history books
and presided over by the intoning of the reporter
who shifts from massacre to massacre
like a tourist leaving me with postcards
that show the colorful objects the dead have made.
Whisper into my ear of how you still live
and what the last blow taught you.

THE STONE OF LANGUAGE

Disappointment Island

Disappointment Island leans into the South Pacific.
The monkeys are still and silent in the trees,
they watch the horizon, their hearts shrink
to the smallest nut, close-lipped shell
they fling down in disgust.
Lizards crawl through the shadows, dig their claws
down to find some treasure, but there is only sand
and their tails follow, eternally erasing their journey.
Birds venture out further and further,
scream at each shape in the water,
but there are only the shadows of clouds passing.
Their calls echo back, fool the birds on shore
to expect exotic visitors,
but when they return home
all goes on as before.
All birds, all insects and fish,
all four-legged mammals,
all with tails and feathers and scales,
all the snakes winding around all the others,
all were hoping someone would come,
something would change,
but nothing happens
and each is locked into his own skin,
dragging his tail over the gritty earth,
singing his heart out in the middle of the night,
miserable over the sameness of the island,
blue sky and water, palms dipping into shadows,
the brilliant flowers blazing and dying and no one
can stop it.
No one comes in a boat,
no one lands from the air,
no one swims in
or is swept onto shore
to lie trembling and dripping with seaweed
before all the inhabitants who raise their arms or wings
or heads from their limbless bodies
to praise the gift the gods have sent
to change everything in the moment of arrival.

Tirza in the Land of Numbers

Little eggskull Tirza, you will hike to your shattering
under the old tired sun,
burning rocks in the hands of boys
burning bullets lodged in the long shaft of darkness
that ends in the hands of soldiers, all that begins
and ends with soldiers' hands
rattles in the blood of their hands
that are equal parts heat and ice.

You bend to lace your hiking boots.
When you rise, a flush of blood
speeds to your head, all light
is in your eyes, you stand
dizzy as you will be
dizzy under the sun and the rocks that strike
at the bright iris, at the deep back
of your skull, where the bullet
enters. You bend

as he without name, reported and forgotten
in a quick slash of ink, bends to his plough
while behind him the furrows fill with his own blood
and that of his unborn children,
and his wife,
still unmarried,
grieves always for her lost soul,
hating the sun and its clear day
and its barbed stream of hikers.

Tirza
the shattering of the thin bone house,
the spilling of blood and more blood,
always hurt me, even when I was little
golden star
like splattered yolk
against my frail chest.

The terrible scales swing wildly night after night
in my skull's darkness, in my opposite eyes,
in my history and my heart, in my warm hand and my cold one,
in my white eyes and the floating landless green
and the blazing black center of each,
the terrible scales swing and knock hard
against the thin membrane over my eyes
and I pile up, on one side, emptiness
and on the other
emptiness.

I cannot bear knowing the language of numbers:
2 Palestinians, Tirza, 123
Palestinians, how many
Jews, 1 Israeli soldier, Sabra
Shatila

Something is wrong in the land of numbers,
Tirza. Your two feet on their hike
into the occupied territories
ring with feet, are filled
with feet, and you, born too recently
to survive, could not hike alone
or even with a few friends.
The land is the land no longer.

The sky's clear pool lies
and all that is on the land lies
and each man lies to the other
and asks the sky for blessing.

At your funeral they call for revenge.
Such prayers crawl slowly over the rocky earth.
They call for revenge as if your death
were first, little eggskull, and sudden,
a shock of rent blue sky,
but what they ask for
has already been done.

Perhaps the woman taking in the sweet clean sheets
from the length of rope until she reached for another
and thought it clean but found it filled
with her own blood,
perhaps, in the language of numbers,
she is your revenge, Tirza,
and you
hers.
Perhaps you lie with the end of yourself,
sheltering an Israeli bullet in your dark last thought,
or perhaps you will have to make room for many others
beneath the droning of a sky
that would hurl your enemies as insects
against the stone cliffs, and you,
its own little daughter,
as nothing at all.

crush

crush
the rushing wind
she crush
the fists of them
who crush
the braided
cherished skull, the girl
sacrifice, the girl face
of morning
the sweet dew that linger
the talk she sing

oh mother
oh rushing wind of mother rush
to the stone to the fist to the
ones who crush the shout of joy
who crush
shine of eye
dream of home
flight of birds
water language
animal shout
softness of boy
warrior memory
girl desire
boy desire
baby happiness
they even try to
crush the sorrow song
crush the gospel word the gospel
truth crush
all the town
and village
and shining sea

oh boat of heart
cracked open
fill
the home with wander
the rags with dance
of millions on the rolling log

destroy!
they who
crush the fish
crush the coral
crush purple heart of shell
hack the rolling log, deny the spirits
flung headlong
into the whisper roar rush
of sea
that pounds the earth
for answer

The Stone of Language

I sit motionless
and all that is sky falls into my lap,
into the momentary body. I will catch
the stone flung, meteorite
on its journey to where life
started, stone of my heart, of my
womb and brain. Across the sky I can see
the way it was: the rain that had no name,
the flower that could not open and be seen,
the green trembling
and the spot of blood.
I can see it, the beginning of the rains
and the flow of the man and the woman,
the tiny blood beginning of girl
who did not know what she was
nor where it would begin inside her
nor what it was called, nor whom.

This rock of time voyages, this song of stone
falls as I am falling
out of myself with the weight of love
thrown back upon itself, the weight
of language singing, singing to itself, forlorn, faceless,
sad mouth, lonely lonely tongue, longing for the god that lives
in the body of the beloved, longing for the community of stars
in the ground of black milk, in the ground of all sadness exhaled
and burning with impossibility, with that longing
we all have.
Under this sky of anger and song and darkness that drenches
us with whispers of the old songs, I am calling out, finally
knowing that no one may answer, I may go back into time
with my whole soul inside my body joined to none other, lingering,
searching for the other side of the mirror, falling through
oceans, living in the sky.

Rock of time, song of stone,
depository of all names and their offspring,
hear me!

I have come from Europe where the dying tree calls out to me,
I remember Africa in the devout beard of my grandfather,
I am pulled down to the carved stone cities of the Indians
by ancient memories of my grandmother, hair of thick black silk,
hair of the field at night, reflecting and containing the sky.
Each root unravels,
each history beats on the window,
crawls my skin to the ancient knot that has
along its pathways
all names, all towns and nations,
all the colors of the people,
the names of their stones and knives,
the animals that feed them,
the quiverings of vegetables,
the beginning of the throat,
the trees whose names I will learn,
birds and their crests of fire
and their crests of the deepest sea
and their crests of the jungle grasses and the tangled leaves.
The knife is on the table. It is kept sharp. Its nature
is to cut.

But to cut the stone of language,
to cut the stone of the heart
that listens deep in its bloody chamber
to the echo of language
and to its deception,
while love falls down the glass to the worn stone floor
eroded by the passage of all pilgrims
who leave marks to be deciphered. All this
in the nature of stone: to wear down,
to be marked, not to break open.

I begin again as I have always begun,
with a rock in my throat and the loveless hand
of another raised against me, raised against us all.
I sing as I study the floor, as I have learned from
those before me, slaves and women, cleaning their own hearts
with the wide sweep of their arms and the foul rag filled
with ugliness. I know no face and sightless
I wander with the stone in my throat
and the raucous birds in the plaza,

the dust of executions
and the softness that exists in the center
of my palms, small secret hearts fluttering in my fists.
O hard days, I have learned how not to break open.
My language too is secret, though my song flies to each ear
and I speak table, chair, rock, limbs circling the heart
and the mouth open down to its birth cry.
I have learned, and I tell anyone easily,
that the densest night cannot be broken open,
that patience must live between the beats of the anguished motor,
between the waves that pass over us, waves of blood
and thin salt water that find us
in the silence of closed fists and curled spine.

All these words to say
I cannot go home.
The trek leads me everywhere,
leaving always another roof hiding my first bed,
leaving always the shadow of a hill
where sperm and egg brought the words of one heart
to another, where the song, ecstatic or forced,
honeyed, shrill, full-throated, hidden,
sang death upon death
of the body and the sobbing open heart.
After I rest within the din of one city or another,
or one chorus or another of grasses and fallen petals,
I must always, with grief and longing, push on to the next,
my hands filled with stones that will split open
only with the right word uttered in the first place
beyond the waters,
before the land had found its molecular structure
and the desire of one atom for another
called out
but could not yet be heard.

The knife is still on the table when I wake up
to hear the evangelist on the television say,
"It is a terrible thing to fall into the hands of
the living god."
I fall into the language of this god,
amplified, televised, spinning,
preaching through child-fanatics, all fear,

filled with the wrath of armies of fetuses,
their tiny fingers pointing, crosses thudding
against frail breastbones.
I dreamt I had a baby, she emerged
alien, wrinkled, tender, with the enormous hands
of a sculptor, no tiny burrowing animal,
no tentative note of hope, but a patient being
floating in a warm bath or lying, contemplative,
on my vacant belly, holding her enormous hands
out to me, waiting for her art to arrive,
her hands already filled with stones.
When I wake to the terrible threat of god,
to the soaring voice of the evangelist who urges
our second birth in the middle of fields of death,
the child, whose existence was sure, who knew me
and had promised me a story, a particular life
unlike any other, is gone, but the knife
is still on the table.

It is time to leave the bed drenched with the labor
of dreams and the hard flight into the past.
Now the hands that opened
are empty, and the soft vision of my sweet aging
explodes into brittle bone and the cell's wild splitting
after one bird call or the ringing telephone,
the full bladder or the fraction of an instant
of unnamed terror
and the holding of the light to one's face
like water to the skin in flames.
O horrible dissipation of the dream
in the instant of reaching for the pen
or reaching for the lover across the gulf between you
when all stops except time itself and then you are only
the one you have had to become.
When I leave, I lock something in,
there in the darkness of my apartment,
in the nightslip collapsed over the chair
or, on the days when the sky is gray and bears down,
on the floor that throbs with the sounds of the apartment
beneath me, if someone listens.

Flight after flight I pass the others.
I have never found a house I could enter.
Each massive door greeted me with silence
or the impatient wail of an infant
and the shrill chorus around her, immigrants shouting
in wonder at the one citizen in their midst
who wails at her double citizenship,
at the clutter of papers on the bureau to identify her,
at the parents whose language will be different from her days
and will not break open.
I could not believe that the stone fist of language
in my throat would bleat like the bloody heart
and yet be seamless, granite, closed
to the instruments I carry, and my pleadings
to the hand above, to the rock within me,
would become all that I own,
beautiful sometimes but closed
to the water, and even, stone heart, closed to the blood.

I move over the map.
I chase the day, its rise and fall, its workers
finding their way to the death that awaits them
in the screaming of metal and machinery
or in the hushed maze of circuitry,
and its farmers
coaxing the grain under the awful faces of bankers
whose oily speeches slip like stones into the bloodstream
until farmers begin to punctuate the rise and fall
of the sun with gunshots:
their families, themselves.
I go to the houses where children lie in rubble
while their parents sit with the magic that enters their blood
to numb the ancient rage or push it to explode.
Babies tossed from windows
sail past my open arms,
the birds chattering at how
like a stone
they hit, and how
unlike stone
they shatter and weep
the colors of sunset.

I have not got one name that makes sense
to all my blood. I am weary of this
and my wild hair shakes with fatigue.
But I cannot cut, although the knife
is on the table, so the voyage is still
before me, and the stark shore not even in sight.

But I am the rock and the name,
the knife and the blood. I am the
darkened house and the deep call of new life.
I am citizen and exile, words that sing
and words that reach Death Row
like silence from under its black hood.
I am the shore and its promise
of water. I am the anguish of the reeds
bent by the wind, broken
by the traveller's boat.

I am alone on the island and when I turn,
before I flee into the forest, I see the gleaming eyes,
I note the strange skin stretched to clothe the silence
that has come to find me,
I flee from the stone heart, as all must.
I am lucky that my legs are long and carry me fast.
The stone, hurled, comes to me,
but I am no longer there.
Not at home, not on the journey.
Silence. Sky.
Laughing bird.

Notes:

"City Poem for Hanuman, the Monkey Scribe":

Hanuman, the Hindu monkey god also revered by many Muslims and Buddhists and especially by the masses, is a devoted servitor to Rama, helping him to crush evil on earth; a master of all branches of knowledge as well as a perfect grammarian and rhetorician; and a manifestation of Shiva, the lord of music. According to one story, he was conceived when the wind god Vayu passed into the body of his mother Anjani through her ear.

(See *Hanuman in Art and Mythology,* by K.C. Aryan and Subhashini Aryan.)

Hanuman is related to the African American Signifying Monkey, a functional equivalent of Esu-Elegbara, of Legba (who has many names)—the divine trickster and divine linguist, translator and master of interpretation, often referred to as a scribe or clerk.

(See first chapter of Henry Louis Gates Jr., *The Signifying Monkey,* Oxford Press, 1988.)

Other relations are the Chinese Monkey King, and Hannubus, the Egyptian dog-faced ape, god of language.

"Work Abroad: Riddles":

Many of the specifics in this poem come from Steven Erlanger's article "A Plague Awaits," in *The New York Times Magazine,* July 14, 1991, about the raging, then yet hidden, AIDS epidemic among heterosexuals in Thailand, "where brothels are a way of life." Since that date, the epidemic has worsened astronomically.

"Commerce: Boys":

In discussing the "connection between Hermes . . . god of the stone-heap and Hermes the trickster and culture hero," Norman O. Brown says "The stone-heaps were a primitive sort of boundary-stone, marking a point of communication between strangers. They were placed . . . at crossroads or some other point on a road where strangers met habitually; in a forest or on some hilltop, both of which in a land like Greece constitute natural boundaries. In . . . cultures where the basic unit of society is not the individual but the family or clan, religious and social institutions were strongly affected by distrust of the stranger. . . . Intercourse with strangers was surrounded with magical safeguards . . . practices . . . associated with the god of the boundary-stone."

From Brown's *Hermes the Thief: The Evolution of a Myth,* Vintage Books, New York, 1969, pages 33-34.

"Brixton Photo":

Brixton is a London neighborhood where many West Indians live. Because of the post-war labor shortage, West Indians were recruited by the British government in the 1950s to emigrate to England to work, the men in the transport system, the women in hospital service, but have been among those hardest hit by unemployment, as well as by police brutality and other forms of discrimination. Brixton has been the scene of much civil unrest.

"Burning":

This poem comes from a family account of the death of my paternal grandfather's sister in the Triangle Shirtwaist fire in New York City.

"Immigrants":

In 1965 a force of more than forty thousand United States Marines invaded the Dominican Republic at Santo Domingo and remained as an occupying army until Joaquin Balaguer, the righthand man of dictator Trujillo against whom the people had risen up, was installed as leader.

Poverty, malnutrition, and repression have continued, as have civil unrest and extensive immigration to the United States and South America to escape conditions at home, with many Dominicans dying during their journeys. Hundreds of thousands of Dominicans reside in New York and surrounding areas, many traveling up and back often between their two homes.

A *baile* is a dance.

". . . *como una viuda*" means like a widow.

"These Snapshots I Have Lost":

Panerai was a death camp located a quiet walk away from a railroad station on the outskirts of Vilnius, Lithuania's capital. About 100,000 people were shot there into ten pits now giving forth sweet grass and wildflowers.

This poem was written some time after a trip to the former Soviet Union in 1987, during the Gorbachev period of *perestroika*, or restructuring, and openness.

"Tirza in the Land of Numbers":

Tirza Porat was a fifteen-year-old Israeli Jew shot to death as she hiked in the occupied territories with an Israeli military guard. Her shooting in the late 1980s followed upon that of a Palestinian farmer mentioned but unidentified by *The New York Times*, and was attributed to Palestinian killers. It was later proven that she had been killed accidentally by one of the Jewish Israeli soldiers.

"The Stone of Language":

"It is a terrible thing to fall into the hands of the living god," according to a television evangelist I overheard. Jonathan Edwards in his sermon "Sinners in the Hands of an Angry God" (1741, Boston) says that the hands of god hold you with abhorrence, "much as one holds a spider," but those hands and his "power and mere pleasure" are all that keeps those not born again from falling into Hell, "that lake of burning brimstone."

Quoted from the sermon as it appears in *The Portable Age of Reason Reader*, edited by Crane Brinton (New York: The Viking Press, 1972), pages 348-356.

3^{09} Gen 5/16 KE